S0-ABD-496

CAMBRIDGESHIRE
The Glorious County

GRAHAM UNEY

HALSGROVE

First published in Great Britain in 2009

Copyright © Graham Uney 2009

All rights reserved. No part of this publication may be reproduced,
stored in a retrieval system, or transmitted in any form or by any
means without the prior permission of the copyright holder.

British Library Cataloguing-in-Publication Data
A CIP record for this title is available from the British Library

ISBN 978 1 84114 878 6

HALSGROVE
Halsgrove House,
Ryelands Industrial Estate,
Bagley Road, Wellington, Somerset TA21 9PZ
Tel: 01823 653777   Fax: 01823 216796
email: sales@halsgrove.com

Part of the Halsgrove group of companies
Information on all Halsgrove titles is available at: www.halsgrove.com

Printed and bound by Grafiche Flaminia, Italy

To Mam and Dad, for
always encouraging me to
follow my dreams.

INTRODUCTION

THE COUNTY of Cambridgeshire is one of stark contrasts. Mile after mile of beautiful open countryside, studded with magnificent cities and delightful villages.

Rolling chalk hills fill the county to the south and west, where Cambridgeshire borders the neighbouring counties of Hertfordshire and Bedfordshire, while flat fenlands stretch as far as the eye can see northwards towards the Wash, and eastwards into the thick forests of Thetford on the Suffolk and Norfolk borders. You tend not to think of woodlands when picturing the variety of landscape forms within Cambridgeshire, but the county enjoys a dramatic backcloth of ancient woods and scrub. Waterways, both natural and man-made provide glorious ribbons of quicksilver slicing through the stunning scenery.

The county is, of course, most famous for Cambridge itself, and its many colleges, while its other city, Ely, is perhaps much less known. (Peterborough is part of the county for ceremonial purposes but is a unitary authority in its own right). Add to this mix a thousand or more market towns, villages, hamlets, and scattered farms, and you get the feeling that this glorious county is very much lived in and loved.

Cambridgeshire also revels in some wonderful watercourses. The River Great Ouse rises far away to the west in Northamptonshire, flows and splutters through Buckinghamshire and Bedfordshire, where it becomes a proper river, then continues in graceful meanders into Cambridgeshire. Some wonderful towns dot the banks of this magnificent river. St Neots lies within a big double-bend – a chicane – of this mighty force.

Huntingdon stands majestically over the serene waters, while a little way downstream St Ives is particularly picturesque. In the north of the county the Nene enters near Peterborough, and flows through the middle of the Fens via the Bedford Levels to pour into the turgid waters of the Wash just north of Wisbech, while possibly the most famous of the county's rivers, the Cam begins life as two main tributaries, the Granta, and the Rhee. The former rises south of Cambridge, just over the border in Essex near Saffron Walden, while the Rhee starts life over the Hertfordshire border near Ashwell. Aside from these natural watercourses, countless dykes, ditches and lodes have been cut through the fens over time, providing a beautiful patchwork of marsh, field and wood.

These diverse and important habitats play host to some of Britain's most interesting wildlife species too, and while this book aims to introduce you to the whole of the county landscape within its pages, I have also included a number of photographs depicting the natural world which forms an important aspect of the Cambridgeshire scene.

Central to the theme of this book are the images of human life and activity within the county. Cambridge itself is, of course, featured, although not too heavily. For that you could take a look at the companion to this book, *Spirit of Cambridge*, which depicts life in that most beautiful of cities. Ely, Wisbech, St Ives, and countless villages, hamlets and farms are here too, showing what a wealth of scenic variety there is within the landscapes and townscapes of Cambridgeshire – The Glorious County.

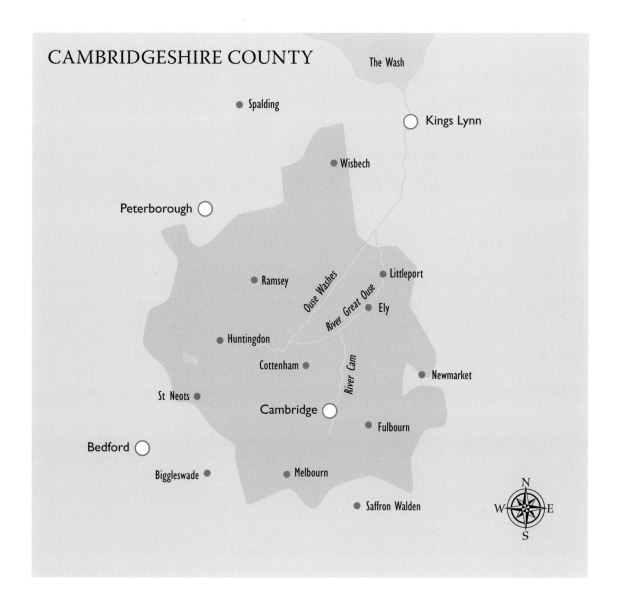

CAMBRIDGESHIRE COUNTY

The Wash

● Spalding

○ Kings Lynn

● Wisbech

Peterborough ○

● Ramsey

Ouse Washes

● Littleport

River Great Ouse

● Ely

● Huntingdon

River Cam

● Cottenham

● Newmarket

St Neots ●

Cambridge ○

● Fulbourn

Bedford ○

Biggleswade ●

● Melbourn

● Saffron Walden

N
W E
S

Cambridge is, of course most famous for its university. Corpus Christi College lies just off King's Parade. Pass through the gatehouse doors and you are confronted by the splendid New Court. The College of Corpus Christi and the Blessed Virgin Mary, to give it its full title, was founded in 1352.

Tucked away behind the colleges are 'The Backs', overlooking the River Cam. Clare College is just one of the many fine buildings that stand on this lovely river.

Pembroke College was founded in 1347 by Marie de St Pol, the Countess of Pembroke, and as such is the third oldest of Cambridge's colleges. Other notable features of the college include the first chapel to be designed by Sir Christopher Wren, and this stunning sculpture of William Pitt the Younger, a fellow of the college who went on to become the youngest British Prime Minister at the age of 24, in 1783.

Trinity College was founded by Henry VIII in 1546, combining the old King's Hall and Michaelhouse. This is the Great Court, with the Great Gate hiding behind The Fountain.

Nevile's Court at Trinity College was built by Thomas Nevile in 1605, and comprised only three sides. The fourth, at the far end of the lawn, is the Wren Library. This was originally just a wall, but was replaced by the library in 1695. The local master mason, used rock from a Rutland quarry, and built the library to a design by Sir Christopher Wren.

Punting on the River Cam at the bridge that leads from
Trinity College along The Avenue.

St John's Street leading towards St John's College. St John's College was founded in 1511 by Lady Margaret Beaufort, mother of King Henry VII. It is the second largest of Cambridge's colleges.

The Round Church on Bridge Street, Cambridge. It was built around 1130 and started life as a wayfarer's chapel. It soon became the parish church of the Hospital of St John, which later became St John's College.

Inside the Round Church on Bridge Street. There are only four remaining round churches in England, and this is a fine example.

Cycling is the most popular form of transport in Cambridge. Trinity Street often has more people passing by on bikes than on foot!

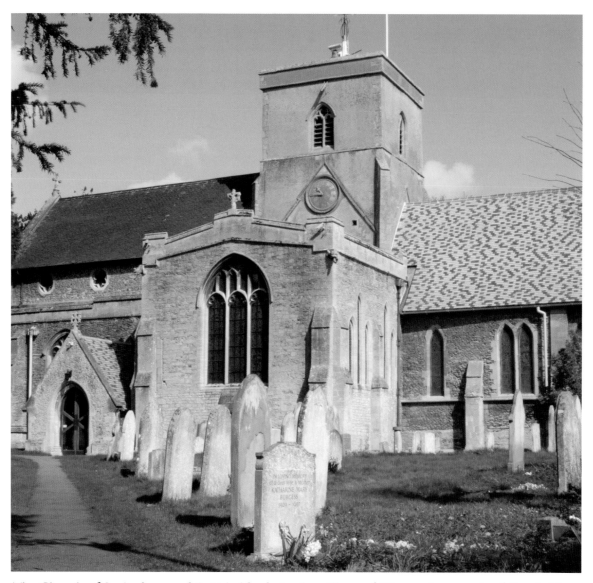

The Church of St Andrew and St Etheldreda in the village of Histon, just north of Cambridge. The present church dates from 1217, but it is known that there was a church on this site at least a century earlier than this.

Histon is a lovely place packed with interesting half-timbered houses, pubs, and shops.

South of Histon lies Impington. This wonderful tower mill dates from around 1805, but replaced an earlier post mill. The mill ceased working around 1929, about the time when the owner, John Chivers, died.

Walk south out of Cambridge and you come to the famous Grantchester Meadows, alongside the River Cam. Here you can sit and picnic while pondering on what inspired local boys, from the original line-up of Pink Floyd, to write a piece about the meadows.

The River Cam at Grantchester village is gorgeous. You can hire a punt from Cambridge to get you to the village, then walk back after taking tea in the famous Orchard where Rupert Brooke, E.M. Forster, Bertrand Russell, and Virginia Woolf would spend afternoons.

The Orchard at Grantchester was first planted in 1868, and became a tea garden in 1897 when a group of Cambridge students asked Mrs Stevenson of Orchard House if they could take tea beneath the delicate blossoms of the fruit trees. Rupert Brooke later lived in the village, and there is a small museum in the car park to The Orchard.

Almshouses at the village of Fulbourn, just on the eastern limits of the city of Cambridge.

Anglesey Abbey is a superb Augustinian priory dating from 1236. Henry VIII dissolved the abbey in 1536, and in the years that followed, the various members of the Parker family, who then owned the site, set about turning the remains into a country home. In 1966 Anglesey Abbey was placed in the care of the National Trust in the will of Lord Fairhaven.

There is a large and very lavish visitor centre, café and shop at Anglesey Abbey, opened in 2008 by Charlie Dimmock.

Robert Green, one of the long-standing gardening team at Anglesey Abbey, works on clearing herbaceous borders in the autumn.

Sculptures are a big feature of Anglesey Abbey, and are often tucked out of the way. This one is hidden in an evergreen hedge.

Another of Anglesey Abbey's sculptures.

Thatched cottages in the village of Lode.

St James' Church in the village of Lode.

Lode takes its name from the fact that it lies at the end of Bottisham Lode, which connects to the River Cam near Waterbeach. A lode is a man-made channel, cut during the draining of the fens.

There has been a mill on the site of the present Lode Mill, overlooking Quy Water, since the time of the Domesday Survey, although the present mill is thought to have been built in the eighteenth century. Lord Fairhaven purchased the mill in 1934, to be used as a focal point to his garden, and it was restored in 1982 by the Cambridgeshire Wind and Watermill Society.

Quy Water runs between the villages of Stow-cum-Quy and Lode, and joins with Bottisham Lode at Lode Mill. It's a great place for a waterside stroll.

The village of Swaffham Prior is dominated by its twin churches, set together on a hill above the High Street. The church of St Mary was built during Norman times, whereas the church of St Cyriac and St Julitta is thought to have existed before 1066. In 1667 a parliamentary order combined the two churches under a single parish.

St Mary's Church in Swaffham Prior.

Foster's Mill at Swaffham Prior was built by local millwrights, Fysons of Soham, in 1857. The mill was owned by the Foster family until they closed it down in 1946. It was restored by Michael Bullied, and grinding corn began again in 1992. The mill is now owned by Jonathan Cook who today produces organic flour, all milled by the power of the wind.

Duxford Chapel is a modest fourteenth-century chantry chapel. Today it is owned by English Heritage, but it is likely that the chapel originally served as a hospital.

The Queen's Head at Newton, surely a contender for the title 'Cambridgeshire's greatest pub'? It is one of the few public houses in Britain to have featured in every single edition of CAMRA's Good Beer Guide! Try the legendary soup, or the fabulous sandwiches, and you'll wonder why you ever go anywhere else for lunch.

The village of Thriplow was said to have around 100 horses in the 1930s, which was enough to keep any blacksmith out of mischief! By the 1990s the old smithy was in a bad state of repair. In 1994 the roof was replaced and the building underwent a complete renovation, although today it appears to have changed very little.

Fowlmere RSPB Reserve is a superb little nature reserve in the south of the county.
Its reedbeds, willow scrub, and woodlands provide a superb habitat for a range of
interesting wildlife species.

Reed buntings sing from the tops of bulrushes, sedges and reed at Fowlmere RSPB Reserve.

Evening at Goffer's Knoll, an ancient bowl barrow near the southern boundary of the county.

At Hyde Hill, at the border of Cambridgeshire near Royston, the sun slips behind a clump of old trees.

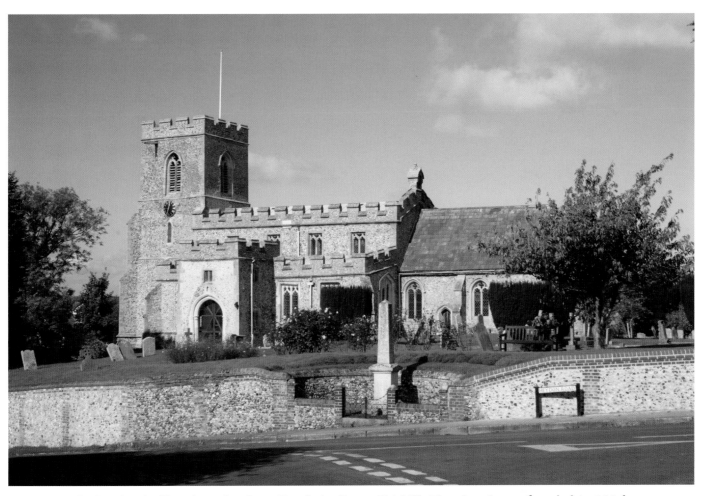

St Swithun's Church at the Cross Roads in Great Chishill. The church was founded in 1136 by Geffrey de Magnaville under the Monastery of Saffron Walden.

One of many lovely thatched cottages in Great Chishill.

Great Chishill itself is the name of the highest hill in the whole of Cambridgeshire. It stands at a mighty 146m (480 feet) above sea level! The hill and village are right in the very south of the county, being only 1 mile from Essex to the east, and 1 mile from Hertfordshire to the west. Until the county boundaries were changed in 1895 the village was in Essex, while today the village has a Stevenage postcode – very confusing!

Muntjac deer have been introduced into Britain via various deer parks,
but escapees from the parks are now widely spread throughout the southern counties.
On the southern fringes of Cambridgeshire, they are a familiar sight.

The Great Chishill post-mill stands to the west of the village on the road to Barley. The first record of a mill appears in 1592 though it is possible there was one there before. The first recorded owners were the Cooke family and the first recorded miller was Joseph Rule in 1677. The Cambridgeshire County Council acquired the Mill in the 1960s, after William Pegram stopped working it in 1951.

Walking on the Harcamlow Way between the villages of Great Chishill and Heydon. This unofficial long-distant route takes walkers on a large figure of eight from Harlow to Cambridge and back. The distance is 140 miles, and it takes in some of the best scenery in southern Cambridgeshire.

The rolling chalk hills of southern Cambridgeshire from near Heydon.

The Litlington Lock-up or Cage was built in the eighteenth century. The petty criminals of the parish would have been held in the cage before they were taken to Court. Before the Rural Constabulary Act of 1839 there were no police as we know them. The law then was enforced by Parish Constables and the Churchwardens. The Litlington Cage is thought to have been last used during the social unrest of the 1840s, when the occupant set fire to the hay that was provided for his comfort. The Cage later became the village pump room.

Looking across fields of barley to the village of Guilden Morden.

Right: An old field barn on the edge of Guilden Morden village.

The church of St Peter and St Paul at Steeple Morden.

Wimpole Hall was built by Thomas Chicheley in the 1600s. Over the centuries the building has changed a good many times, the most notable alterations being carried out between 1713-1732 by James Gibbs. Later, in the 1790s the remarkable yellow drawing room was added by Sir John Soane, and this room is still considered by many to be one of the most extraordinary in any country house in Britain.

In 1976 Mrs Elsie Bambridge bequeathed the Wimpole Estate to the National Trust, including the fabulous Gothic Tower that looks over the Serpentine Lakes at the Chinese Bridge.

Exploring the fields,
meadows and
woodlands at
Wimpole Hall.

In 2003 shire horses were returned to Wimpole Home Farm, and are now used to provide wagon rides between Home Farm and the Hall.

A delightful thatched cottage in the village of Little Eversden.

The earliest record we have of the open trestle post mill at Bourn is from 1636, but it may be much earlier as this design of windmill has hardly changed since the thirteenth century. In 1932 this mill was given to the Cambridge Preservation Society. Being one of the oldest surviving mills in the country, it is now a scheduled ancient monument.

Looking up the sails of the Great Gransden post mill.

Even older than the Bourn post mill is the one at nearby Great Gransden. It dates from 1612, and is the oldest post mill in England.

The Paxton Pits Nature Reserve was created in the 1985 when Huntingdonshire District Council collaborated with the aggregate companies who had quarried sand and gravel here since the 1930s. Together with local conservation bodies, anglers, and water sports clubs, they produced the Ouse Valley Recreation Local Plan, which included the establishing of a Local Nature Reserve at Paxton Pits.

A common tern fishing at Paxton Pits Nature Reserve. These graceful birds nest on the reserve, and are a wonderful sight during the summer months.

Perhaps the most exciting thing about Paxton Pits today is that it's very much a reserve in the making. The Huntingdonshire District Council have agreed a plan with Aggregate Industries to continue extraction of the remaining gravel beds to the north of the reserve, and Cambridgeshire County Council's Mineral Planning Authority have passed these plans on the understanding that there will follow a phased release of the newly quarried land over the next ten years.

A little way downstream along the Great Ouse is Houghton Mill. In its mid-nineteenth-century heyday, the mill ran 10 pairs of stones, powered by three separate waterwheels. Much of the internal machinery remains intact although the wheels were removed in the 1930s when the mill stopped production. Today, corn is ground by a pair of millstones powered by the north waterwheel which was re-instated by the National Trust in 1999.

Mute swans nest on the River Great Ouse at Houghton.
Here a cob has six young cygnets to look after.

The Three Horseshoes pub at Houghton, a welcome drinking hole for those boating on the nearby Great Ouse.

St Ives on the River Great Ouse. In ancient times St Ives was the furthest point inland that was easily navigable by sea-going vessels, and it was this that made its ancient international markets and fairs so important – these events brought wealth and prosperity to the town and also to nearby Ramsey Abbey.

Looking up the River Great Ouse from the Chapel on the Bridge in St Ives,
towards All Saints' Parish Church.

Bridge Street in St Ives.

The fine waterfront in St Ives. The abbots of Ramsey Abbey had inherited the right to collect tolls for using the bridge at St Ives to cross the river. Back then, the name of the town was Slepe, but Abbot Ednoth had an idea to increase the popularity and income of the town. He acquired the bones of Saint Ive, a Bishop from Persia, and brought them to Slepe so that pilgrims could visit his saintly remains, and the name of the town was changed.

The Chapel of St Ledger, otherwise known as the Chapel on the Bridge, in St Ives was built during the construction of the stone river bridge in the early fifteenth century. Records show that the chapel altar was consecrated in 1426. What actually went on in the chapel is a matter of conjecture but we know that at the time of the Dissolution the last Prior of St Ives was allowed to live out his days in the building.

Modern housing on the river in St Ives.

Right: At Fen Drayton the RSPB have a superb nature reserve
right on the banks of the Great Ouse. The reserve was created
from old sand and gravel extraction pits.

Wading birds are common at Fen Drayton RSPB Reserve, and at the right time of year you might be lucky enough to spot a green sandpiper.

Looking across the fields to the east from Fen Drayton RSPB Reserve, the most obvious feature is the old tower mill at Swavesey. This is Hale Mill, and it replaced an earlier post mill in 1866.

The Crown at Broughton is a fine example of a village pub being brought back from the brink of closure. It was bought by the community in 2001, and now under a new landlord, is considered to be among the finest gastro-pubs in Cambridgeshire.

The barman at the Crown in Broughton, serves a fine pint of real ale while superb gastronomic delights are rustled up in the kitchen.

Wistow Fen Lane leads downhill to Wistow Fen and Turf Fen. The Cambridgeshire Wildlife Trust manage a small woodland reserve here at Wistow Wood, and this is one of the few sites in Cambridgeshire where rare woodland butterflies have been recorded, such as the black hairstreak.

Right: Ramsey, the site of the old Ramsey Abbey.

St Thomas à Becket Church at Ramsey. The church was part of the original abbey at Ramsey, and was converted from a hospital in the early part of the twelfth century.

Today little can be seen of the once grand Great Benedictine Abbey of Ramsey. In its heyday it was the most important abbey in the Fens, being home to over 80 monks, and being the wealthiest abbey for miles around. The abbey was dissolved in 1539 by Henry VIII, and it fell into Cromwell's hands. The abbey was destroyed, leaving only this gatehouse and a long stone wall.

Village cottages in Ramsey.

The modern windmills of the Fens. These wind turbines are a major feature for anyone driving over the Bedford Levels near Chatteris.

Woodwalton Fen National Nature Reserve lies at the lowest point of East Anglia. It will form part of the Great Fen, an exciting project to link together a number of fens to form a huge 3000 hectare site.

Holme Fen National Nature Reserve will also become part of the Great Fen. Holme Fen was once the site of Britain's largest lowland lake, and now, after years of peat cutting and fenland drainage in the area, it is clothed with silver birch, making it lowland Britain's biggest woodland of its type.

A speckled wood butterfly, common throughout woodlands in Cambridgeshire.
Holme Fen is a great place to look for this species.

The Holme Fen Post. In 1852, a cast-iron post was erected by William Wells at the edge of Holme Lode covert. The top of the post was set at ground level and the rest buried and fixed to timber piles driven into the underlying clay. Since then the peat has dried out and washed away due to drainage of the fens. The current position of the post shows how much the ground has shrunk in the last 150 years. The farmland adjoining the reserve is now the lowest place in Britain.

Holme Lode, one of the many drainage ditches cut across Holme Fen.

Thorney Abbey in the North Levels. In 972, an abbey was re-founded on the site by St Aethelwold and it soon became the centre of a major fenland estate.

The village post office in Thorney.

In the north of the county the River Nene cuts across the Bedford Levels and takes a turn northwards at Wisbech, towards the Wash.

Houses on North Brink in Wisbech, some of the finest Georgian buildings in England. The North and South Brinks were built by eighteenth century landowners, merchants and warehouse owners. The Brinks are split by the River Nene.

North Brink in Wisbech. The Georgian houses of The Brinks have featured in many TV productions and films, and were described by Pevsner as 'the most perfect Georgian streets in England'.

Right: Allison Napier, the Head Gardener at Peckover House, works in autumn pruning espalier pears.

Far right: The sundial in the gardens at Peckover House.

Left: Peckover House on North Brink is owned by the National Trust. It was built in 1722 and bought by Jonathan Peckover at the end of that century. The Peckovers presented the building and its superb walled gardens to the Trust in 1948.

Mulberry the cat at Peckover House. There's a long tradition of naming the cats of the house after fruit trees!

The Orangery at Peckover House, a fine, quiet corner of the garden.

Ann Gaughan, serving a careership as a gardener at Peckover House, tidies up the herbaceous border.

The old stables at Peckover House.

On South Brink in Wisbech is the birthplace of Octavia Hill. Hill was born in 1838, and she went on to become one of the three founder members of the National Trust, in 1895. Octavia's greatest achievements however were concerned with housing reform. She worked tirelessly to improve housing for the poorest people of society, particularly in London.

The Norman Castle in Wisbech was replaced by a Bishop's Palace in 1478, and again by a mansion house in the seventeenth century, built for John Thuloe, Oliver Cromwell's Secretary of State. The current building is a Regency villa, built in 1816.

The Wisbech and Fenland Museum contains some surprising artefacts, including Napoleon's breakfast service, Louis XIV's ivory chess set, and the original manuscript of Dickens' *Great Expectations*.

The Crescent at Wisbech was developed by local builder, Joseph Medworth, in 1816.

An old sign on the corner of The Crescent in Wisbech.

Wisbech was originally a medieval port, but when the estuary of the Great Ouse silted up, the river was diverted into the Wash at King's Lynn. The present course of the River Nene was then constructed from Peterborough to Wisbech. Today there is a thriving yacht harbour on the cut at Wisbech.

On Laddus Fen, just south of Wisbech, a disused line of telegraph poles stretches into the distance.

The Fens are, of course, great arable lands. Here, a farmer picks leeks near Friday Bridge.

The Fens are also important for wildlife. A young kestrel perches on a telegraph pole, waiting for his next meal to come by.

At Laddus Fen the old course of the River Nene moves sluggishly through the flatlands.

The Sixteen Foot Drain cuts through Upwell Fen, straight as an arrow.

Wind turbines on Euximoor Fen near March.

Central to the story of Ely Cathedral is St Etheldreda, a Saxon princess converted to Christianity. As Queen of Northumbria, she married twice. Etheldreda is honoured as a virgin saint, despite her previous marriages, and she remained as abbess at Ely from AD673 until her death in AD679. In 1081 work began on a new cathedral, and much of what we see today dates back to that time.

Ely Cathedral's West Tower.

The magnificence of Ely Cathedral can best be appreciated on one of the many tours.

The only major feature of Ely Cathedral that is of a later date is the Octagon Tower, which was built to replace the original Norman tower, which collapsed in 1322.

A signpost in Ely, advertising the Stained Glass Museum in the Cathedral.

Right: The Stained Glass Museum in the Cathedral is well worth a visit in its own right, although you can combine this with a tour of one of the towers.

Church Lane sign in Ely.

The Gallery sign in Ely.

Oliver Cromwell came to Ely before his rise to political fame during the English Civil Wars of 1642 – 1649.
When he lived in the city, from 1636 until 1647, he was known as the Farmer of the Tithes.
Cromwell's house is now a museum.

The Old Fire Engine House in Ely is now an art gallery and restaurant, although it was built in the eighteenth century on the site of the home of Dean Tyndall's widow.

The Prince Albert Pub in Ely is a
fine place for a pint of local real ale,
good, simple food,
and captivating conversation.

Ely stands on the River Great Ouse, and is a busy place today with boat owners, and day-trippers.

Modern cabin cruisers and a boat-lift at the marina in Ely.

Narrowboats at Ely on the Great Ouse. There's a superb network of rivers, lodes, and channels throughout the fens for boat owners to explore.

A lovely way to explore the fens around Ely is by following
the waymarked trail, the Fen Rivers Way.

The River Great Ouse at
Ely at dusk.

The Dutchman, Sir Cornelius Vermuyden, working for the Duke of Bedford, undertook massive drainage work that ultimately led to the landscape of the fens we see today. Here the New Bedford River, or Hundred Foot Drain, was cut to take water directly to the sea, rather than following its natural course along the River Great Ouse.

Left: Until the draining of the fens in the seventeenth century, Ely was very much an 'island of eels', being surrounded on all sides by treacherous marshlands, over which only the foolish would try to cross without the aid of a local guide, or 'fenslodger'.

121

The Old Bedford River is cut alongside the New Bedford, and together they form an oasis of wet meadows known as the Hundred Foot Washes. The RSPB, Wildfowl and Wetlands Trust, and the Cambridgeshire Wildlife Trust all have important nature reserves on these washes.

122

A blue-tailed damselfly on the Hundred Foot Washes.

Looking north along the Counter Wash Drain towards the pumping station at Paradise Farm near Mepal.

In the village of Witcham stands St Martin's Church.

The name Witcham comes from 'wych-elms' which used to grow there in abundance. The village lies on the Isle of Ely, which before the fens were drained, was indeed an island.

The Hall at Witcham.

On the River Great Ouse stands the Stretham Old Engine, a fine
example of a land drainage steam engine. It was the first of its
kind, being built to replace the old windpumps in the draining of
the fens in 1831.

Right: One of the older-style drainage pumps, a windpump at
Wicken Fen National Nature Reserve.

James Selby, the Reserve Warden at Wicken Fen
National Nature Reserve, and Val Horspool,
Volunteer, clear reeds from Thompson's Drove on the
edge of Sedge Fen.

A common frog at Wicken Fen.

One of the secluded pools at Wicken Fen. Wicken Fen was the very first nature reserve to be owned by the National Trust, and it remains in their safe hands today.

A great crested grebe at Wicken Fen National Nature Reserve.

Shaun Walters working at reed clearance on Mitchell's Drove at Wicken Fen.

Tubney Fen near Reach is now in the care of the National Trust also.
It is part of the grander scheme known as the Wicken Fen Vision.

A common hawker dragonfly at Tubney Fen.

The Maid's Head public house in Wicken village.

Apart from the windpump on Wicken Fen, there is another windmill tucked away behind the village houses. The Wicken Corn Mill was built in 1813, and was used to grind wheat until the 1930s. It was restored in 1987 by a local preservation group, and is now a superb example of a smock mill.

The smock and sails of the
Wicken Corn Mill.

The automated gates of the lock leading into
Reach Lode from the River Cam.

Reach Lode is one of the quieter waterways in East Anglia.

Dusk on Reach Lode.

The River Cam at dusk near Upware.

The quiet solitude of life in Upware.

William and Mary cottages on the High Street in Chippenham. The village was built largely to house estate workers from Chippenham Park.

Cross outside the church in
Chippenham village.

Isleham lies in the south-east corner of Cambridgeshire.
St Andrew's Church dominates the centre of the village.

The River Lark forms the boundary of Cambridgeshire to the east, with Suffolk being on the opposite bank. The Riverside Isleham Marina is a pleasant place to enjoy a waterside walk.